MALCOLM **X**

Rights Activist and Nation of Islam Leader

MALCOLM X

Rights Activist and Nation of Islam Leader

BY TOM ROBINSON

CONTENT CONSULTANT
ALAN BLOOM
ASSOCIATE PROFESSOR OF HISTORY
VALPARAISO UNIVERSITY

ABDO
Publishing Company

CREDITS

Published by ABDO Publishing Company, PO Box 398166, Minneapolis, MN 55439. Copyright © 2014 by Abdo Consulting Group, Inc. International copyrights reserved in all countries. No part of this book may be reproduced in any form without written permission from the publisher. The Essential Library™ is a trademark and logo of ABDO Publishing Company.

Printed in the United States of America,
North Mankato, Minnesota
052013
012014

Editor: Megan Anderson
Series Designer: Becky Daum

Photo credits: Eddie Adams/AP Images, cover, 2; Robert Parent/Time Life Pictures/Getty Images, 6; Pan American Airways/AP Images, 11; Shutterstock Images, 16; AP Images, 18, 24, 60, 69, 87, 91; Library of Congress, 20, 50, 57, 59, 76, 78, 81; Walter Sanders/Time Life Pictures/Getty Images, 28; Time Life Pictures/Getty Images, 33; Hulton Archive/Getty Images, 35; John Tresilian/NY Daily News Archive/Getty Images, 38; Chris Ross/NY Daily News Archive/Getty Images, 42; Peter Keegan/Keystone/Getty Images, 45; Robert L. Haggins/Time Life Pictures/Getty Images, 49; Paul Cannon/AP Images, 64; Matty Zimmerman/AP Images, 70; Pictorial Parade/Getty Images, 74; John Lent/AP Images, 83; Richard Saunders/Pictorial Parade/Getty Images, 88; Edward Kitch/AP Images, 94

Library of Congress Control Number: 2013932923

Cataloging-in-Publication Data

Robinson, Tom.
 Malcolm X : rights activist and nation of Islam leader / Tom Robinson.
   p. cm. -- (Essential lives)
 ISBN 978-1-61783-893-4
 Includes bibliographical references and index.
 1. X, Malcolm, 1925-1965--Juvenile literature. 2. Black Muslims--Biography--Juvenile literature. 3. African Americans--Biography--Juvenile literature. 4. African American civil rights workers--Biography--Juvenile literature. I. Title.
 320.54/6/092--dc23
 [B]   2013932923

CONTENTS

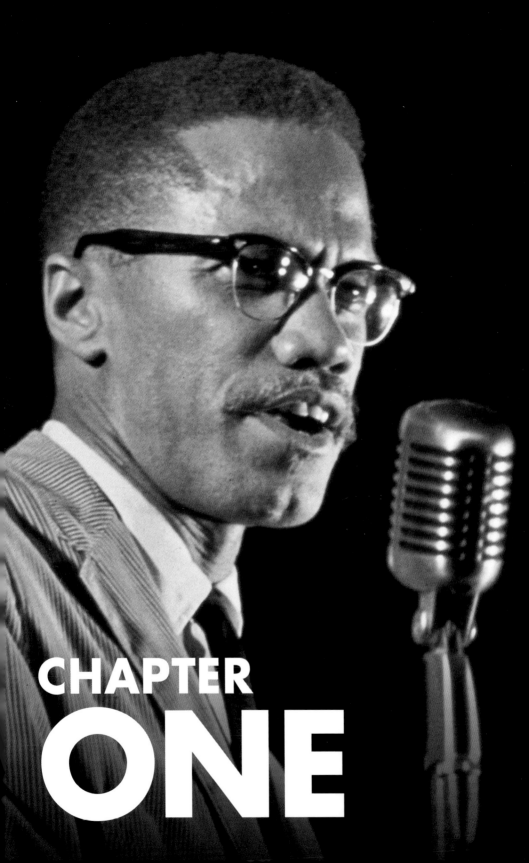

CHAPTER
ONE

BY ANY MEANS NECESSARY

Malcolm X stepped up to the podium on June 28, 1964, at the Audubon Ballroom in Harlem, New York. Fresh off his trip to Africa and Mecca, Saudi Arabia, Malcolm X had a new organization to promote. He was ready to introduce the latest step in his ongoing efforts within the American civil rights movement of African Americans, as well as his work for global human rights.

While away, Malcolm X had decided to create the Organization of Afro-American Unity (OAAU). He was prepared to make his first speech as leader of the OAAU to explain how his worldviews had evolved. Neatly dressed in a suit, a white shirt, and a thin, dark tie, Malcolm X settled himself behind a waist-high podium that supported a variety of microphones. His head down, he soaked in the warm applause. With a nod

A charismatic and persuasive speaker, Malcolm X commanded the attention of his audience.

Mecca, in western Saudi Arabia, is the holiest city in the Islamic religion. The prophet Muhammad, the founder of Islam, was born in Mecca. Mecca is approximately 45 miles (72 km) from the Red Sea coast, surrounded by the Sirat Mountains.

Devout Muslims turn toward Mecca five times each day in prayer. They attempt a religious pilgrimage there at least once in their lifetime, providing they have the financial means and the absence does not create a hardship for their families.

from Malcolm X, the applause quieted and the audience was seated.

As Malcolm X formally greeted attendees, he acknowledged the presence of friends and enemies. He had collected plenty of both as an outspoken activist for civil rights during a time when race issues were especially volatile in the United States.

A New Vision

The OAAU and its first meeting were the latest representations of Malcolm X's often-controversial effort to gain recognition, respect, and fair treatment for African Americans. He first gained fame for his work within the Nation of Islam, a group of Muslim African Americans united under the religious teachings of its leader, Elijah Muhammad. After Malcolm X began following Muhammad, he became one of the Nation of Islam's most active ministers, spreading its religious message to its followers, also known as Black Muslims, around the country.

Malcolm X's public mission started out as a religious one. As he pursued better treatment of blacks in the United States, his mission began to deal with political issues. The Nation of Islam, however, often sought to avoid political involvement while pursuing a goal of separating blacks from white America.

To explain his vision for the OAAU, Malcolm X began by saying his intention in leaving the Black Muslim movement was to also work with the 22 million non-Muslim African Americans. He wanted to create an organization to study the problems of African Americans and determine whether to form a Black Nationalist party. Black Nationalism is a social movement supporting the idea of keeping black Americans separate from white Americans, rather than integrating multiple races into one society. A Black Nationalist party would work to give blacks more control of their local economies and governments by promoting this separate identity from whites.

Malcolm X had transitioned more toward achieving global human rights. He explained he was reaching beyond Islam and seeking a better life not just for

African Americans, but colonized populations around the world as well. He first described his religious pilgrimage to the Islamic holy city of Mecca. He then explained how he attempted to gain a better understanding of African-American problems while spending time in Africa. "Our African brothers have gained their independence faster than you and I here in America have," he said. "They've also gained recognition and respect as human beings much faster than you and I."[1]

During his visit to Africa, Malcolm X said he was able to study the work of the Organization of African Unity (OAU), which was created in Ethiopia in 1963. It united African people in their efforts to eliminate colonialism on the continent. "Once we saw what they were able to do, we determined to try and do the same thing here in America among Afro-Americans who have been divided by our enemies."[2]

Having witnessed how the OAU helped create a cultural movement among African people, Malcolm X developed a more global perspective. He was inspired to bring this pursuit of human rights, advancement, and progress to the United States through the OAAU. He said:

Malcolm X returned from a view-changing trip to the Middle East and Africa on May 21, 1964.

Just ten years ago on the African continent, our people were colonized. They were suffering all forms of colonization, oppression, exploitation, degradation, humiliation, discrimination, and every other kind of -ation. And in a short time, they have gained more independence, more recognition, more respect as human beings than you and I have. And you and I live in a country which is supposed to be the citadel of education, freedom, justice, democracy, and all of those other pretty-sounding words.[3]

Malcolm X praised the OAU and noted how Africans with opposing views had been willing to set aside their differences and meet to find solutions for a common cause.

The Motto

Malcolm X's address that night was another example of the charisma he brought to public speaking and his skill at energizing those with a common cause. Preaching with rich and rhythmic words, Malcolm X knew how to keep an audience interested, whether it was a religious congregation or a political rally. The crowd in Harlem remained quiet as Malcolm X spoke, then responded with cheers as he concluded each point.

Malcolm X said the objective of the OAAU was to bring complete independence by any means necessary to people of African descent in the United States and all of the Western Hemisphere. It soon became clear "by any means necessary," was the central theme of his speech:

> We want freedom by any means necessary. We want justice by any means necessary. We want equality by any means necessary. . . . We don't think that we should have to sit around and wait for some segregationist congressmen and senators and a president from Texas in Washington, DC to make up their minds that our people are due some new degree of civil rights. No, we want it now or we don't think anybody should have it.[4]

Malcolm X ultimately uttered the phrase "by any means necessary" nine times during his speech, as well as "whatever means necessary" twice, and eight other references to necessary. The impact of these words made Malcolm X's speech in Harlem that night an enduring part of his legacy, even a half century after his death.

What Malcolm X meant by "by any means necessary," however, was open to interpretation. Malcolm X was clear in other parts of the same speech that violence was sometimes necessary. He advocated self-defense rather than being a victim, the way many blacks were viewed at the time. Some viewed "by any means necessary" as a threat. Others looked at the word *necessary* as Malcolm X's way of saying violence was sometimes a necessity. Malcolm X spoke about the importance of self-defense as a guiding principle of the OAAU. "We assert that in those areas where the government is either unable or unwilling to protect the lives and property of our people, that our people are within our rights to protect themselves by whatever means necessary," he said.[5]

MAN OF MANY NAMES

Malcolm X was known by more than one name during his lifetime. At birth, in 1925, he was named Malcolm Little. During his wilder times in the early 1940s, while living and working around the entertainment industry in New York City, Malcolm Little often answered to the nickname "Detroit Red" because of his red hair.

After he was released from prison and converted to the Islamic religion in 1952, he changed his name to Malcolm X. The *X* stood in place of his family name, which was lost among the generations after slaves were brought to the United States and took the names of their owners.

The completion of a religious pilgrimage, or hajj, in 1964 led to his final name change, el-Hajj Malik el-Shabazz. Following his death, Malcolm's wife, Betty, and his children went by the surname of Shabazz.

Malcolm X told the audience it was not unlawful or immoral for African Americans to prepare to or actually defend themselves. He said:

> Tactics based solely on morality can only succeed when you are dealing with people who are moral or a system that is moral. A man or system which oppresses a man because of his color is not moral.[6]

While discussing necessary means, Malcolm X's speech also addressed important, long-term issues, including the need for better education. He emphasized to young blacks that their history was not made up entirely of former cotton pickers, but also prominent, successful men and women who played a significant role in the nation's development. He spoke of the importance of having better job opportunities and housing. Malcolm X implored those in attendance to take responsibility for reducing crime in their own communities rather than relying on the police or government. He also discussed African Americans becoming more politically active, particularly by voting.

A Place to Start

Malcolm X said he chose Harlem as the place to start the OAAU because of its concentration of Africans.

The Audubon Ballroom became the Malcolm X and
Dr. Betty Shabazz Memorial and Education Center in 2005.

He compared being African in Harlem to ethnic white
neighborhoods where people identified themselves as
Irish, Italian, or German, rather than American. He
emphasized the movement needed to spread beyond the
United States. Afro-American, to him, meant people
in all of North America, Central America, and South
America who had African blood. Malcolm X's goal was
to unite all those people in a quest for a better life.

The civil rights movement had often been split.
It involved a debate over whether African Americans
should integrate into US society as it was or segregate

themselves from those who might never recognize them as equals. Although Malcolm X was often in the middle of this debate, he also knew the importance of unity.

Many of the goals Malcolm X envisioned took shape after his death. He was assassinated while speaking at the Audubon Ballroom just a year later. His experiences growing up in the United States during a time when equal rights were a topic of heated debate—and a dream still regularly being fought over—helped shape the focus of his life.

AUDUBON BALLROOM

The Audubon Ballroom was the site of Malcolm X's "By Any Means Necessary" speech, as well as his 1965 assassination. Located at Broadway and 165th Street in the Washington Heights section of New York City, it was built in 1912 as a multipurpose entertainment center.

During the years following Malcolm X's assassination, the Audubon began to deteriorate. Many residents and Malcolm X supporters tried unsuccessfully to have the Audubon Ballroom designated and preserved as a New York City landmark. Several New York City organizations managed to complete a $7 million renovation in 1995. A portion of the site reopened on May 19, 2005, on what would have been Malcolm X's 80th birthday. It was renamed the Malcolm X and Dr. Betty Shabazz Memorial and Education Center, with the goal of educating the public about Malcolm X's life and mission.

CHAPTER
TWO

VOLATILE CHILDHOOD

Malcolm Little was born on May 19, 1925, in University Hospital in Omaha, Nebraska. He was the fourth child of Earl Little Sr. and his second wife, Louise. Malcolm joined older siblings, Wilfred, Hilda, and Philbert. Earl also had three children from his first marriage.

Malcolm's parents met while they were both members of the Garvey movement, which was named after Jamaican Marcus Garvey. Garvey had started the Universal Negro Improvement Association (UNIA). Like other followers of the movement, Earl and Louise were known as Garveyites. The couple married in May 1919 and moved around often while helping organize UNIA chapters in many cities throughout the United States. Their work involved many of the religious and civil rights concepts that eventually became a big part of Malcolm's life.

Tragedy and racism in Malcolm's childhood would later shape his activism.

Garvey's philosophy supported Black Nationalism
and uplifting people of African descent.

Earl and Louise moved to Omaha from Philadelphia,
Pennsylvania, with their oldest son, Wilfred, in 1921.
Activity of the Ku Klux Klan (KKK), a Protestant-based
hate group that terrorized blacks with its violence, was
reaching its peak in Nebraska in the mid-1920s.

The Littles were often targets of KKK violence. Louise later told Malcolm that while she was pregnant with him, hooded KKK members approached the family's home in Omaha with shotguns looking for Earl. During another incident, Klan members broke the windows of the family's home.

Earl and Louise eventually moved their children to Milwaukee, Wisconsin, where many young African-American families were moving for jobs as laborers. The Littles had another son, Reginald, before moving their family on to East Chicago, Indiana.

THE GARVEY MOVEMENT

Marcus Garvey was born on August 17, 1887, in Saint Ann's Bay, Jamaica, but came to the United States in 1916. Garvey had started the Universal Negro Improvement Association (UNIA) in Jamaica in 1914, to uplift and unite all people of African ancestry. When he arrived in the United States, Garvey saw growing discontent among blacks, particularly those who had emigrated from colonies in the Caribbean. Blacks had become more and more disillusioned after deadly race riots in East Saint Louis, Missouri, in 1917, and the lack of improvements following World War I (1914–1918). Garvey started the first UNIA chapter in New York City in 1917. Garvey was a gifted speaker and promoted the idea of black self-reliance, including racial unity and economic independence. He is credited with starting and championing the concept of "black is beautiful." Garveyism concepts provided the roots of future Black Nationalist movements. Garvey was deported to Jamaica in 1927 after being charged with US mail fraud. He never returned to the United States and died in London, England, in 1940.

Malcolm's parents moved around a lot, before and after they were married. In fact, they met in Montreal, Canada, even though neither was from Canada.

Earl was born on July 29, 1890, in Reynolds, Georgia. He left school after just three years, but learned carpentry as a teenager. "Early," as he was known, married his first wife, Daisy Mason, in 1909. After trouble with his in-laws and local whites, he left his wife and family behind. He spent time in Philadelphia and New York City before settling in Montreal.

Louisa Langdon Norton was born in Saint Andrew, Grenada, an island in the Caribbean, in 1897. Called Louise, she was raised by her maternal grandmother, Mary Jane Langdon. At 19, Louise left Granada for Montreal, seeking better job opportunities.

Scary Night

In 1929, the Little family purchased a farmhouse outside Lansing, Michigan. But they were unaware local laws excluded blacks from owning property in the area. Malcolm's parents fought in court to be able to keep their home.

As the legal battle ensued, the home caught fire on November 8, 1929. The fire department, though reportedly called, never responded, and the house burned to the ground. Earl said he had seen white men dousing the home in gasoline and setting it on fire.

Escaping the fire was an early memory that stuck with the children. Malcolm's older brother Wilfred, who was eight at the time of the fire, said he remembered hearing a "big boom." Wilfred later recalled in *Malcolm X: Make It Plain*, a 1994 PBS documentary:

> When we woke up, fire was everywhere. . . . I could hear my mother yelling, my father yelling. And they made sure they got us all rounded up and got us out.[1]

As his home on the outskirts of Lansing burned, Earl fired a shot at what he later said were arsonists escaping the property. There was plenty of evidence of a racial motive behind the fire. But the police investigated Earl in connection with the blaze, which had destroyed his home and threatened the lives of his family.

Two insurance policies, valued at $2,000 and $500, were considered as possible motives for Earl to burn down his home. Earl was denied the insurance money as lengthy investigations ensued. Earl was charged with possession of the unregistered handgun he had used the night of the fire.

Family Tragedy

Malcolm often accompanied Earl when his father spoke at UNIA functions. He later shared his memories from the time he was five and went with his father, remembering, "The meetings always closed with my

The KKK used cross burnings to terrorize black communities.

father saying several times and the people chanting after him, 'Up, you mighty race, you can accomplish what you will!'"[2]

Earl's activism had made him a constant target of those opposed to African-American causes. On September 28, 1931, Earl left the family home in Lansing, Michigan, to collect money from the sale of some chickens and never returned. Police woke Louise in the middle of the night with news that Earl had been the victim of a horrific accident—he had been run over by a streetcar.

By the time Louise could make it to his bedside at the hospital, Earl had bled to death from multiple injuries. Earl's death was officially ruled an accident by the Lansing coroner and reported as such by the local newspaper. But family members and many blacks in the area believed the KKK had been involved.

Malcolm later described how constant hate crimes against his family had haunted his childhood. He blamed the KKK for these incidents, as well as his father's death.

A Separated Family

Malcolm's life went through dramatic changes after his father's death. Louise struggled with mental health problems following the loss of her

THE KU KLUX KLAN

White southerners formed the hate group known as the Ku Klux Klan (KKK) in 1865, following the Civil War by white southerners who opposed equality for blacks. The KKK used intimidation and violence to advance its belief of white supremacy. The group is particularly known for its white hoods, demonstration marches, and burning of crosses. The group targeted blacks, Catholics, Jews, and others who did not fit into its Protestant roots.

The KKK's influence grew during the early part of the 1900s. Malcolm often blamed his father's violent death on the Black Legion, a group that had split from the KKK during the 1930s. The KKK gained momentum again in the 1950s and 1960s, during the civil rights movement. Now existing as mostly independent, splintered chapters, the KKK is estimated to have between 5,000 and 6,000 members as of 2012.

husband. With the family on welfare, state social workers visited often. Malcolm had begun stealing from markets in Lansing when he was hungry. Social workers placed him in foster care with a local family in 1937.

Louise was ultimately determined insane and confined to the Kalamazoo State Hospital on January 31, 1939. Wilfred and Hilda were old enough to stay in the family home. Louise's other five children were sent to live with three other families, but they all remained in contact with one another.

Ella Collins, Malcolm's half sister from his father's earlier marriage, arrived from Boston, Massachusetts, after hearing of the family troubles. Ella spent time helping Wilfred and Hilda, and also arranged for all of the siblings to visit their mother together, before heading back to Boston.

About a year later, the State of Michigan determined Malcolm should be raised in the Ingham County Juvenile home in Mason, Michigan. This cut back on opportunities for Malcolm to visit his siblings.

Despite the turmoil in his life, Malcolm was thriving as a student at West Junior High School in Lansing. He was popular but, as the only black student in his grade, he later described this popularity as being treated like a mascot. Having success in school allowed Malcolm to dream about his future.

Malcolm began talking with Richard Kaminska, his English teacher, a white man who Malcolm had looked up to, about becoming a lawyer. But Kaminska discouraged him and told him, "You've got to be realistic about being [black]. A lawyer— that's no realistic goal for a [black man] . . . Why don't you plan on carpentry?"[3]

In 1940, Malcolm traveled to Boston to spend the summer with Ella. While there, he decided he had had enough of Michigan. In February 1941, 15-year-old Malcolm boarded a Greyhound bus and took the daylong ride to Boston, seeking a fresh start.

SIBLINGS

Earl and Louise had seven children. The oldest was Wilfred (1920), followed by Hilda (1922) and Philbert (1923). After Malcolm was born, they had three more children, Reginald (1927), Wesley (1928), and Yvonne (1929). Louise also had another son, Robert.

Earl also had three children with his first wife, Daisy Mason: Ella (1914), Mary (1915), and Earl Jr. (1917). Never officially divorced from Daisy, Earl left her and their children behind in Georgia after eight years. Malcolm did not know about or spend time with his half siblings until he was a teenager.

CHAPTER THREE

LIFE OF CRIME

Ella brought her younger half brother Malcolm from Michigan to Boston to live with her in 1941. In Ella, Malcolm had found a caring, older family member upon whom he could rely. "She was the first really proud black woman I had ever seen in my life," Malcolm said.[1]

Though, perhaps unintentionally, Ella showed Malcolm where to find trouble. By the time Malcolm came to live in Boston, Ella had developed criminal tendencies, including shoplifting. Frequently operating on the fringe of trouble, Ella had been arrested 21 times in 20 years. But out of those brushes with the law, she was only convicted once.

Various Jobs

Malcolm had quit school before he headed to Boston. Ella helped him find a job shining shoes at the Roseland Ballroom. A seemingly endless string of jobs followed. While working at the Roseland Ballroom, Malcolm

Malcolm got a job shining shoes at the Roseland Ballroom, a dance club in New York City.

ODD JOBS

From the time Malcolm quit school as a teenager until he went to prison at age 20, he had many jobs. In addition to shining shoes at Roseland Ballroom while in Boston, he was also a bartender and nightclub entertainer. While in Lansing, Michigan, Malcolm worked at a jewelry store, as a messenger, and as a ballroom dancer.

In 1943, after moving to New York City, Malcolm also worked as a waiter at Small's Paradise, one of Harlem's most well-known and successful nightclubs. It was especially popular during the 1920s and 1930s, and a favorite spot among many Harlem writers, poets, and artists.

also found less formal—and illegal—ways to make money. He worked in the men's room on dance nights, and some customers would look for more than a shoeshine. They would ask for places to find liquor and drugs, among other things. Malcolm found out being the source paid better than shining shoes.

Malcolm progressed into a life filled with crime. He sold drugs, was a runner for illegal gambling, and was involved in a series of burglaries. Some believe Malcolm exaggerated these years of lawlessness in his public speaking to help emphasize his message of change through religion. But Malcolm clearly had been living outside the law.

After becoming familiar with the streets of Boston, Malcolm found kitchen and food service jobs on trains traveling between Boston, New York City, and other major cities in the Northeast. Stops in Washington, DC, left Malcolm astonished at the level of poverty in some black neighborhoods in the nation's capital.

With help from a newfound friend, trumpet player Malcolm "Shorty" Jarvis, Malcolm found a connection to the entertainment and nightclub scenes. This in turn gave Malcolm places to sell drugs. Malcolm was a showman in his own right. He dressed flashy and stood out in a crowd. Such a lifestyle, however, required money. The pursuit of money meant Malcolm ventured into even more criminal activity.

In 1943, at an age when he still should have been in high school, Malcolm relocated to Harlem, a large black

DETROIT RED

Malcolm was known around Harlem as "Detroit Red," because of his reddish hair. Malcolm also got his name because he was from Michigan, and Detroit was a more familiar city than Lansing. Detroit Red was a character in his own right. He wore flashy clothes, including zoot suits, which had long, wide-shouldered jackets and pants with wide, cuffed legs. He knew how to attract attention, particularly by having his hair "conked," a chemical process removing the natural kinks or curls in a black person's hair, to make it straight and shiny.

Other red-haired, black men in Malcolm's circle went by similar names. Between 1942 and 1944, Malcolm worked on and off at Jimmy's Chicken Shack with John Elroy Sanford, who was known as "Chicago Red." Sanford went on to find fame as comedian Red Foxx, and starred in *Sanford and Sons*, a popular 1970s television sitcom.

neighborhood in Manhattan, a borough of New York City. Malcolm was drafted to serve in the US Army during World War II (1939–1945) when he turned 18 in 1943. On the day of his assessment, Malcolm dressed and acted as outrageously as possible. During his assessment by a military psychiatrist, Malcolm kept up his wild act. Malcolm was declared 4-F, which meant he was unfit for military service.

Malcolm's life of crime, however, was starting to catch up with him. He was often fired from his jobs. Sometimes, he got them back. Other times, he moved on to another.

Arrests

Malcolm was charged with larceny in November 1944 in Massachusetts and received a three-month suspended sentence as well as probation. He returned to Michigan at the beginning of 1945, where he started working as a busboy. But on March 17, 1945, Malcolm was arrested and charged with grand larceny for robbing a man he knew from Detroit, Douglas Haynes, at gunpoint. Malcolm's brother Wilfred posted his bail. While awaiting trial, Malcolm fled the state and returned

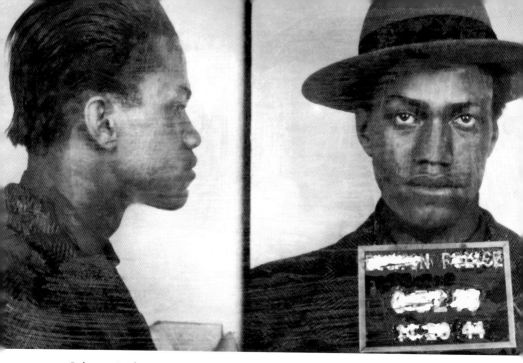

Police in Roxbury, Massachusetts, charged Malcolm with larceny in 1946.

to Boston. Later that year, a warrant was issued for Malcolm's arrest.

Jarvis and other friends joined Malcolm to pull off a series of burglaries of rich homes in the Boston area in late 1945 and early 1946. Police closed in on the group. When Malcolm returned to a repair shop to pick up a stolen watch he had left to be fixed, police were ready to arrest him for the latest theft. Malcolm was caught carrying a loaded pistol, adding to his troubles. Police convinced him to give up the names of the others in his theft ring.

But the court process did not go well for Malcolm and Jarvis. They both pled guilty to multiple crimes and each received eight- to ten-year prison sentences from Middlesex County, Massachusetts.

State Prison

Not yet 21, Malcolm started his prison sentence at the Charlestown State Prison in Charlestown, Massachusetts, on February 27, 1946. During his early days in prison, Malcolm's record as a prison worker was not much better than his days as a civilian worker. He was more interested in selling and trading cigarettes to other prisoners than performing the jobs required of prisoners. He often had conflicts with guards.

But another inmate encouraged Malcolm to use his time behind bars to educate himself. Malcolm became an avid reader and spent a lot time in the prison library.

PRISON LIFE

Malcolm spent time in three different Massachusetts facilities during the nearly six and a half years he served of his eight- to ten-year sentence. Malcolm started at Charlestown State Prison February 27, 1946, and was transferred to the Concord Reformatory in Concord on January 10, 1947. In 1948, after less than a year and a half, Malcolm was moved to Norfolk Prison Colony in Norfolk. At Norfolk, Malcolm gained access to an extensive library to continue his studies.

While in prison, Malcolm began writing to
Nation of Islam leader Muhammad.

Malcolm studied the dictionary, memorizing the definitions of words. He took classes through state-sponsored correspondence courses and received his high school diploma.

A New Outlook

While studying in prison, Malcolm discovered the Islamic religion. Another prisoner told him about a group called the Nation of Islam, which was led by Elijah Muhammad and combined Islamic teachings with Black Nationalist beliefs.

NATION OF ISLAM

Wallace Fard founded the Nation of Islam in the early 1930s. The Nation of Islam combined concepts of the Islamic religion with Black Nationalism. Beginning in the 1960s, members of the Nation were also sometimes referred to as Black Muslims.

When Fard disappeared in 1934, Elijah Muhammad, formerly Elijah Poole, became the leader of the Nation. Under Muhammad, the Nation grew in stature. Muhammad continued Fard's teaching that Islam was closer to the roots of black people, who had been introduced to Christianity by white people. Muhammad often appealed to convicts, because they had been disillusioned by life in the United States either before or during their time in prison.

Nation members read the Koran, worshipped Allah, and were expected to follow strict religious rules. Muhammad emphasized black pride. The Nation preached reliance on other African Americans. By building their own support structure, they could be less reliant on white people, who had once held them as slaves.

Malcolm's brother Reginald had also joined the Nation of Islam's Temple No. 1 in Detroit. Reginald told Malcolm about the Nation. Other family members had also joined the Nation while Malcolm was still in prison.

During his transition to his new religion, Malcolm began living a more disciplined life. The former drug user quit smoking and gambling. And in keeping with the dietary restrictions of Islam, he no longer ate pork.

Malcolm also began corresponding with Muhammad. He nervously wrote several drafts of his first correspondence. Eventually, he wrote to Muhammad every day, committing to lifestyle changes and seeking guidance. This connection would shape much of the rest of his life.

CHAPTER FOUR

THE NATION OF ISLAM

On August 7, 1952, Malcolm X was released from the Massachusetts state prison system. Before he left prison, Malcolm had converted to the Nation of Islam. Once released, Malcolm chose not to answer to Malcolm Little. He took the title Malcolm X in protest of the idea his name came from the days of slavery, rather than from his family's roots in Africa. "My father didn't know his real name," Malcolm X explained about his name change, something common among Nation members. "My father got his name from his grandfather and he got his name from his grandfather and he got it from the slave master."[1]

As Malcolm later learned, the Nation of Islam shared many of the teachings of traditional Islam, but also had some major differences. The Nation of Islam taught its founder, Fard Muhammad, was the reincarnation of Allah, or God. Fard Muhammad, who started the

Malcolm X left prison in 1952 a changed man.

Nation in Detroit in the 1930s, disappeared in 1934.

The Islamic religion teaches Allah's message was carried through prophets. Leader Elijah Muhammad, originally Elijah Poole, was viewed as a prophet by the Nation, but not by other Muslims. The Nation of Islam also built much of its recruitment around blacks and other nonwhites. Belief in traditional Islam, however, is not based on race.

Starting Over

Malcolm X had become a different person in more than just his name. During his time in prison, he had also overcome an addiction to drugs and studied to make himself more educated. He left prison dedicated to strict lifestyle changes in order to adhere to his new religious beliefs.

Within days of his release from prison, Malcolm X moved to a Detroit suburb to live with his older brother Wilfred and Wilfred's wife, Ruth, for the remainder of 1952. Malcolm X began each day by praying to Allah and eventually joined the Nation's Detroit temple.

Malcolm X also met with Muhammad. Malcolm X moved to Chicago, Illinois, in 1953 to live with Muhammad and study the teachings of the Nation's spiritual leader. Malcolm X was asked to speak at the Nation of Islam's Detroit temple about what Muhammad's teachings had done for him. Malcolm X's commitment to the Nation's cause grew deeper, and soon he completed his training as a minister. He began working to spread the word of the Nation.

Following Muhammad's advice, Malcolm X recruited young blacks with the hope older black members would follow. Before being assigned to his own temple, Malcolm expanded the Nation's membership by visiting bars and nightclubs around Detroit, looking for people he could recruit. Blacks who were poor and disillusioned with life in the ghettos of US cities were commonly drawn to the Nation's message.

Muhammad appointed Malcolm X the chief minister of Nation of Islam Temple No. 11 in Boston

Rising quickly through the Nation ranks, Malcolm X became minister of Temple No. 7 in Harlem in 1954.

in September 1953. Malcolm X then became minister of Temple No. 7 in Harlem in June 1954. Muhammad also relied on Malcolm X for assistance in setting up temples in Hartford, Connecticut, and Philadelphia, Pennsylvania. Malcolm X was often sent wherever

Muhammad saw opportunities to grow membership. Malcolm X proclaimed Muhammad's teachings, commonly using the phrase, "Elijah Muhammad teaches us . . ."[3] With a persuasive speaking style, Malcolm X's delivery of Muhammad's message was often more effective than hearing Muhammad himself.

Charismatic Nation Minister

Malcolm X helped increase the membership of the Nation. He drew new members with his passion and delivery. "I had never heard a black man in my life talk the way this brother talked," said Louis Farrakhan, who would later become leader of the Nation.[4] Farrakhan studied Malcolm X's speaking style on his way to taking over leadership.

During a time of racial tension in the United States, Muhammad presented the Nation as an alternative to Christianity, which he described as a white man's religion. Malcolm X became more prominent within the Nation as it was experiencing massive growth. Between 1952 and the end of the decade, the Nation grew from 400 to 40,000 active members.

Malcolm X also helped spread the Nation's message with the written word. He eventually started a national newspaper, *Muhammad Speaks*, in 1960.

Controversial Message

While working in New York, Malcolm X was interviewed by the Federal Bureau of Investigation (FBI). The FBI had opened a file on Malcolm X after he described himself as a Communist in a 1950 letter he wrote to President Harry S. Truman from prison.

THE HATE THAT HATE PRODUCED

Public awareness of the Nation and Malcolm X increased with the 1959 PBS documentary *The Hate That Hate Produced*. The documentary aired from July 13 to July 17 in five half-hour episodes. Louis Lomax, a black journalist, joined journalist Mike Wallace in the report.

The series offered a controversial portrait of the Nation and its ideas surrounding racism. Although much of the report was viewed as a negative look at the Nation, the Nation's leaders did see the value in publicity. In an attempt to respond to the report, Malcolm X established *Muhammad Speaks*, a monthly publication reporting on issues from the Nation's perspective. *Muhammad Speaks* was distributed both inside and outside the organization in an effort to promote the Nation's positions.

The Hate That Hate Produced also brought fame to all involved. Wallace eventually gained national recognition and was assigned to cover the 1960 presidential campaign. He later landed a prominent, long-term reporting job on the respected CBS newsmagazine *60 Minutes*. Lomax followed the Nation throughout his career and wrote several books about the organization.

Muhammad Speaks was another way the Nation spread its message.

Now the FBI was keeping an even closer eye on Malcolm X, and began planting undercover officers inside the temples where he ministered.

Muhammad preached Islam was the native religion of blacks before they were brought to the United States as slaves. He taught Islam was only for black people. His message combined Islamic principles with Black Nationalist beliefs. Muhammad encouraged his followers to separate themselves from the rest of America, particularly its oppressive white power structure.

This message sparked new attention from the FBI. Malcolm X's description of whites in power was also perceived as a threat by law enforcement. He was known to describe whites as "blue-eyed devils."[5] Presentations by the Nation, particularly Malcolm X, inspired those who felt powerless, while causing anxiety among those in power.

Spurred to Action

The Nation's position on civil rights was a reflection of Muhammad, who was a proponent of black separation. But Malcolm X showed he was capable of uniting blacks to potentially alter, rather than avoid, the power structure.

One incident in Harlem on April 26, 1957, started his transition from being a religious leader to becoming more active in civil rights. Two New York City police officers were beating an African-American man with nightsticks. Johnson Hinton and two other Nation members were passing by and tried to stop the attack. The officers, however, started to attack Hinton and struck him in the head several times. All four men were arrested and taken into custody.

After word spread of the incident, Malcolm X led a group that marched to the Twenty-Eighth Precinct. There, Malcolm X demanded to see the prisoners. The crowd grew to approximately 500, at which point police allowed Malcolm X to see Hinton. Observing Hinton's condition, Malcolm X demanded Hinton receive medical treatment.

Police transported Hinton to a nearby hospital. The crowd outside the precinct, which included Nation members and others who had gathered from the neighborhood, continued marching on to the hospital. As they made their way through the streets, the crowd grew.

Hinton was returned to the police station after he was treated at the hospital. The crowd continued growing, once again in front of the precinct, igniting police concerns of a major race riot. After arranging a meeting with police officials, Malcolm X made the Nation's position clear. He said:

BETTY SANDERS

Betty Sanders was born May 28, 1936, in Detroit. Betty attended Tuskegee Institute, a black college in Tuskegee, Alabama. She left Tuskegee for nursing school in New York, where she became a nurse. Betty met Malcolm X at a Nation of Islam temple when she was 20. Betty later became known as Betty Shabazz until her death in 1997.

Following her husband's death, Betty continued her education while raising their six daughters. She earned a bachelor's degree in public health education and a master's degree in early childhood education from Jersey State College, then a doctorate in education administration from the University of Massachusetts at Amherst.

Betty became director of communications and public relations, then director of institutional advancement at Medgar Evers College in Brooklyn. She also made frequent public speaking appearances.

We do not look for trouble. . . . We do not carry knives or guns. But we are also taught when one finds something that is worthwhile getting into trouble about, he should be ready to die, then and there for that particular thing.[6]

Once Malcolm X was satisfied his demands were being met, he dismissed the crowd with a wave of his hand. All four men were eventually released on bail. Though all were charged, none were convicted. It was clear Hinton was in need of serious medical attention and his condition was life threatening when he returned to the hospital. The incident led Hinton to receive the largest police brutality lawsuit judgment ever awarded in New York City at the time.

Malcolm X and his wife, Betty, had six daughters.

While lecturing at Harlem's Temple No. 7 in 1956, Malcolm X met Betty Sanders, a nurse who was invited to Nation meetings by an older coworker. After meeting, Betty and Malcolm X started dating, and Betty soon joined the Nation. Inspired by the Nation, Betty eventually became Betty X.

In late 1957, Malcolm X told Muhammad he intended to marry Betty. On January 12, 1958, Malcolm X called Betty from a pay phone at a gas station in Detroit and proposed to her. Two days later, a justice of the peace married Malcolm X and Betty in Lansing. The couple settled in Queens, New York, and welcomed their first daughter, Attallah, in November 1958.

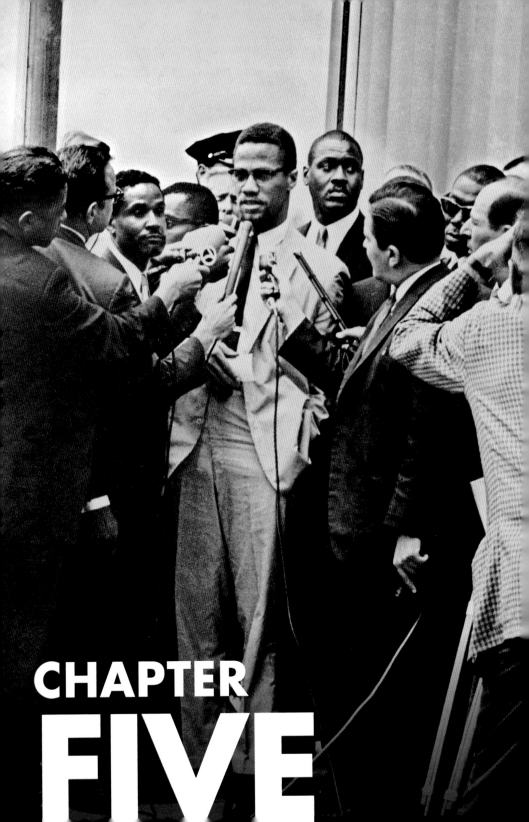

CHAPTER
FIVE

OPPOSING MESSAGES

The Nation and Malcolm X each enjoyed a higher profile as the 1950s drew to a close. The membership of the Black Muslim movement was soaring. In 1959, Malcolm X made his first trip overseas to tour Muslim countries. He made visits to Egypt, Saudi Arabia, Sudan, Nigeria, and Ghana. During his tour, Malcolm X served as Nation leader Elijah Muhammad's ambassador.

With a much more effective speaking style than the more subdued Muhammad, Malcolm X was often the Nation's more visible speaker. In 1961, Muhammad appointed Malcolm X the national representative of the Nation. The appointment caused criticism from members of the Nation's inner circle, who were threatened by Malcolm X's growing profile within the Nation. It also sparked speculation Malcolm was looking to take over the Nation.

By the early 1960s, Malcolm X became more outspoken about civil rights issues.

As criticism and speculation among Nation leadership increased, both Muhammad and Malcolm X seemed to have solutions. Muhammad reassured Malcolm X his fame was a good thing, because it helped spread the Nation's message. He said he understood the natural growth of criticism that came with fame. "You will grow to be hated when you become well known," Muhammad said to Malcolm X.[1]

Fight for Civil Rights

With racial conflicts simmering, Malcolm X was becoming more and more outspoken. He appeared more frequently in debates, and was asked to speak at prestigious colleges.

Compared to other civil rights leaders of the time, particularly Dr. Martin Luther King Jr., Malcolm X held starkly different views on race relations. King and Malcolm X, however, shared some common goals. Both sought to improve conditions for African Americans in a country where just 100 years earlier they had been kept as slaves. But the two men differed on how to achieve those goals.

King advocated a nonviolent approach toward civil rights for African Americans. His goal was to one day achieve equality for blacks who had been living within the country's white-dominated power structure.

One way King sought civil rights was through peaceful bus boycotts in Montgomery, Alabama, in the mid-1950s, when whites in the South refused to adjust to changes in laws aimed at ending segregation. Similar protests led to violent reactions. The civil rights movement had become increasingly volatile

DR. MARTIN LUTHER KING JR.

Dr. Martin Luther King Jr. was a Baptist minister from Atlanta, Georgia, and a key leader of the United States civil rights movement in the 1950s and 1960s. The son of a Baptist minister, King was a member of the executive committee for the National Association for the Advancement of Colored People (NAACP). The NAACP was the largest organization working for black interests at the time.

King led African Americans in protesting Southern segregation laws. He led the bus boycott in Montgomery, Alabama, which started on December 5, 1955, and lasted for 381 days. King traveled millions of miles to make more than 2,500 public speeches in support of civil rights.

King was named *Time* magazine's Man of the Year in 1963. A year later, at age 35, he became the youngest person to ever receive the Nobel Peace Prize. King donated the $54,123 he received with the award to programs supporting the civil rights movement.

The attention King received for his protests led to violence against him, including the bombing of his house. King was assassinated on April 4, 1968, while standing on the balcony outside his motel room in Memphis, Tennessee. He had been in Memphis leading a protest supporting striking city garbage workers. King was 39, the same age Malcolm X was when he was assassinated three years earlier.

DIFFERENT APPROACH

Dr. Martin Luther King Jr. led nonviolent protests against white Americans and businesses refusing to allow blacks equal rights. On the other side were the Nation and Malcolm X, who came along with more radical forms of protests.

Malcolm said his approach made whites appreciate King's approach. Coretta Scott King said in an interview years later that Malcolm X referenced this when she met him in Selma, Alabama, in 1965, shortly before he was assassinated. King was involved in protests there and arrested. Malcolm had spoken and riled up the crowd at a Selma church. Afterward, he told Coretta he was not in Alabama to make trouble for her husband. Rather, he said, when white people viewed the alternative of his more demonstrative approach, they might be more willing to listen to what King had to say.

after members of the National Association for the Advancement of Colored People (NAACP) and other civil rights workers were killed in the early 1960s.

Malcolm X was critical of the nonviolent approach advocated by King. Malcolm X was not afraid to use loud and aggressive methods to ensure blacks were heard on civil rights issues. He encouraged racial pride and called for blacks to defend themselves if attacked.

As the national representative for the Nation, Malcolm X promoted Black Nationalism, which aligned with Nation leader Muhammad's beliefs that blacks in America should live separately from whites. Muhammad wanted blacks to find strength by building their own nation within a nation. As Malcolm became more involved in political debates, he began to veer off the path set by Muhammad. Muhammad was so resistant to political involvement he was against Nation members registering to vote.

The Nation initially appealed mostly to blacks who were tired of inequality and its resulting poverty. When change was slow in the South, the Nation began to attract wealthier blacks as well. Malcolm X kept his teachings consistent with the Nation's message of distrusting white Americans.

Malcolm X and King

King and Malcolm X were well aware of the fundamental differences in their beliefs. During an interview with author Alex Haley, who collaborated on Malcolm X's autobiography, King said,

> I know that I have often wished that he would talk less of violence, because violence is not going to solve our problem. And in his litany of articulating the despair of the Negro without offering any positive, creative alternative, I feel that Malcolm has done himself and our people a great disservice.[2]

Not afraid to criticize mainstream civil rights leaders, Malcolm X said blacks needed to be cautious of

King and Malcolm X greet each other before a press conference in 1964.

black leaders who worked with the white establishment
to achieve civil rights causes. He later used King's 1964
Nobel Peace Prize as an example. "If I'm following a
general, and he's leading me into a battle, and the enemy
tends to give him rewards, or awards, I get suspicious
of him," Malcolm X said. "Especially if he gets a peace
award before the war is over."[3]

Malcolm X's approach left a lasting impact on black
culture. "King was a political revolutionary; Malcolm
was a cultural revolutionary," said James Cone, author of
Martin & Malcolm & America. "Malcolm changed how black
people thought about themselves. Before Malcolm came

along, we were all Negroes. After Malcolm, he helped us become black."[4]

Malcolm's style made him more inclined to offer harsh criticism. At times, however, both men offered reasonable assessments of the other's approach. They even conceded there was no way to be certain their own approach was best. King later acknowledged Malcolm was "very articulate" and may have had "some of the answer."[5] Malcolm also wrote about his differences with King. He said:

> The goal has always been the same, with the approaches to it as different as mine and Dr. Martin Luther King's non-violent marching, that dramatizes the brutality and the evil of the white man against defenseless blacks. And in the racial climate of this country today, it is anybody's guess which of the "extremes" in approach to the black man's problems might personally meet

ONE MEETING

Malcolm X and Dr. Martin Luther King Jr. met in person just one time. Both were in Washington, DC, on March 26, 1964, to attend hearings for the Civil Rights Act. The Civil Rights Act ended segregation in schools and added specific laws against discrimination based on race, ethnicity, and gender.

Malcolm X listened as King spoke in a conference room at the US Capitol. After King's speech, the two men crossed paths in the hallway. They stopped, shook hands, and exchanged polite greetings as photographers snapped pictures. Their meeting was estimated to have lasted less than a minute.

a fatal catastrophe first—"non-violent" Dr. King, or so-called "violent" me.[6]

At times, King and Malcolm X were highly critical of each other's positions. It can be argued, however, as they aged, their views moved closer to one another's. "I know Martin had the greatest respect for Malcolm," said Coretta Scott King, King's widow, in an interview years later. ". . . I think that if Malcolm had lived, at some point the two would have come closer together and would have been a very strong force."[7]

Malcolm X met King in Washington, DC, during hearings for the Civil Rights Act in March 1964. Just weeks later, on April 3, Malcolm delivered another of his most famous speeches, "The Ballot or the Bullet." The famous speech showed a change of course for Malcolm, who said, "It'll be Molotov cocktails this month, hand grenades next month, something else next month. It'll be ballots, or it will be bullets."[8]

Acknowledging "ballots" and the political process as a possible answer was just one way the speech departed from earlier themes. Malcolm X made a specific point of emphasizing he was not antiwhite. "I am anti-exploitation and anti-oppression," he said.[9]

Malcolm X's outspoken views on civil rights
left an impact on black culture.

CHAPTER
SIX

GROWING TENSIONS

Malcolm X was clearly a favorite of Nation leader Elijah Muhammad for years. The bond between the two was so strong it caused jealousy among Muhammad's children and others in the movement's national leadership. The bond between Muhammad and his vocal minister was not, however, unbreakable.

Muhammad often brushed aside questions from within the Nation about whether Malcolm was trying to gain too much attention for himself. He occasionally instructed Malcolm on how to temper his remarks. When necessary, Muhammad gave Malcolm orders about what subjects he could not address publicly.

As he grew in stature, Malcolm did not always strictly follow orders from above. It was one of many issues that created tension between Muhammad and Malcolm. Malcolm X's loyalty had always helped him overcome any philosophical differences with

By 1960, tensions were growing between Malcolm X and other Nation of Islam ministers.

Muhammad. Embarrassing comments by Malcolm X angered Muhammad, whose improper actions eroded the previously unquestioned respect he received from Malcolm.

Controlled Message

Even as his profile grew, Malcolm X demonstrated his loyalty to Muhammad by being careful to turn attention back to the Nation leader. Another Nation minister, Louis Farrakhan, said it was a statement of respect:

. . . it was Brother Malcolm who started referring to Elijah as 'the Honorable' Elijah, and who started making us say . . . 'Messenger Elijah Muhammad taught me' or 'Messenger Elijah Muhammad teaches us. He was driving the point home that Elijah Muhammad was a messenger of God.[1]

Muhammad eventually instructed Malcolm X to avoid making political statements in his college appearances. Malcolm's public appearances continued to spread Muhammad's views on Black Nationalism and Islam. Another indication of Muhammad's concerns was the lack of coverage of Malcolm X's speeches was almost nonexistent in *Muhammad Speaks* during 1962. This was a departure from previous coverage of Malcolm X's speeches in the paper.

On April 27, 1962, the Los Angeles, California, police raided the local Nation temple after a street brawl. Officers opened fire in the temple, shooting seven Nation members, paralyzing one and killing temple secretary Ronald Stokes.

In response, Malcolm wanted to organize volunteers to stand up against police brutality. He made plans to head for Los Angeles. Muhammad, however, ordered him to stay put. Muhammad said Allah would deliver justice for Stokes's death. But Malcolm was frustrated by Muhammad's lack of action.

As a result of the incident, an angry Malcolm showed poor taste when an airplane crashed in France on June 3, 1962. It resulted in the deaths of 121 wealthy white people from the Atlanta, Georgia area. Malcolm X

Even as their relationship became strained,
Malcolm X emphasized his loyalty to Muhammad.

implied it was justice for the incident in Los Angeles,
calling it "a very beautiful thing."[2] While speaking,
Malcolm said, ". . . we call on our God—He gets rid of
120 of them."[3]

Later in 1962, Muhammad released a public
statement, giving Malcolm some leeway to address
political issues. The statement read:

> As long as we are not allowed to establish a state or
> territory of our own, we demand not only equal justice

under the laws of the United States, but equal employment opportunities, now![4]

Malcolm used this limited amount of freedom to rally for causes of poverty-stricken blacks in Harlem.

Challenged Faith

Malcolm X had first heard rumors about extramarital affairs between Muhammad and his Nation secretaries during the mid-1950s. But Malcolm disregarded those rumors as false. In 1963, however, the rumors resurfaced. Malcolm heard the affairs had resulted in Muhammad fathering as many as eight illegitimate children.

Malcolm X discussed the rumors with Muhammad's son Wallace. Wallace confirmed the stories about his father. Malcolm relayed the concerns to another Nation

REUNITED

After a quarter century apart, Malcolm X reunited with his mother, Louise Little, in the fall of 1963. Malcolm and his brother Philbert traveled to Kalamazoo, Michigan, and arranged for Louise's release from Kalamazoo State Hospital.

Malcolm told biographer Alex Haley he was reluctant to talk about his mother being committed. But he later described to Haley what it was like to a have dinner with his mother for the first time in 25 years. "He certainly didn't want to talk about it, because he did not feel good about it," Haley said. "But he felt so great when he and his brother came together to have their mother released."[5] Malcolm and Philbert helped set Louise up in Philbert's Lansing home. Louise Little died in 1991.

minister, Louis Farrakhan, who warned Malcolm he felt obligated to report the conversation back to Muhammad. The shared knowledge further strained Malcolm's relationship with Nation leaders.

As a result of the revelations, Malcolm was less and less comfortable placing Muhammad on a pedestal. This personal assessment of Muhammad's character was combined with a growing awareness of how the Nation varied from traditional interpretations of Islam. Malcolm's teachings in 1963 continued to shift even further toward social and political issues and away from the religion. Although their rift was growing, Muhammad still showed his support for Malcolm. He assigned Malcolm to help fix problems in the Nation's Washington, DC, temple on April 25, 1963.

Muhammad and Malcolm, the Nation's two most powerful men, made their last public appearance together in Philadelphia on September 29, 1963. At the appearance, Muhammad elevated Malcolm from national representative to national minister, a ranking above all other Nation ministers. Muhammad told the crowd present, "This is my most faithful, hard-working minister. He will follow me until he dies."[6]

Suspension

US President John F. Kennedy was popular among blacks. Malcolm had previously compared being black in America to being a prisoner in a racist system. In his analogy, he referred to Kennedy as the warden. When Kennedy was assassinated on November 22, 1963, Muhammad instructed all Nation ministers to refrain from public comments about the president.

Nine days after the president's death, Malcolm took Muhammad's place as a speaker at an event in New York City. As he was instructed, Malcolm avoided the subject of the president's assassination during his speech. However, Malcolm went against

DEDICATION

Even as a rift grew between Malcolm X and Muhammad in 1963, Muhammad professed his allegiance to his mentee. Malcolm X had been busy working on his autobiography with author Alex Haley during the time his relationship with the Nation was falling apart. Still, Malcolm X was sure to praise Muhammad as he wrote the book's dedication.

The dedication, which was never published, read:

This book I dedicate to The Honorable Elijah Muhammad, who found me here in the muck and mire of the filthiest civilization and society on earth and pulled me out, cleaned me up, and stood me on my feet, and made me the man I am today.[7]

The removal of the dedication was part of the final adjustments of the manuscript. Haley had made many changes to the manuscript as Malcolm X's views began to change, as well as after Malcolm's death.

Muhammad's instructions when he answered a question about the assassination. He said the shooting in Dallas was "chickens coming home to roost."[8] Making matters worse, Malcolm added, "Being an old farm boy myself, chickens coming home to roost never did make me sad. They've always made me glad."[9]

Some in attendance tried to minimize the offensiveness of Malcolm's remarks, and Malcolm later accused the media of trying to trap him. For a nation

FAMOUS FOLLOWERS

In addition to reaching poor blacks in cities around the United States, Malcolm X had a way of appealing to celebrities. He connected with author and poet Maya Angelou, actor Sidney Poitier, the first black man to win an Academy Award, Pro Football Hall of Famer Jim Brown, and singer Sam Cooke, among others.

Malcolm also struck up a relationship with budding boxing superstar Cassius Clay, who took the name Muhammad Ali when he converted to Islam. During his suspension from the Nation, Malcolm spent time with the boxer, who was preparing for his famous 1964 fight with Sonny Liston.

Malcolm even hoped adding Clay as a member would help bring an end to his suspension for insensitive public comments about the assassination of President Kennedy.

Clay defeated Sonny Liston to remain undefeated and take the world heavyweight championship. Clay converted to Islam and became a Nation member, but at the same time he broke away from Malcolm. He was under pressure to choose allegiance between either Malcolm X or the Nation. Following Malcolm's death, Muhammad Ali said, "Malcolm X was my friend and he was the friend of everybody as long as he was a member of Islam."[10]

Malcolm X speaks at a rally in Harlem in 1963.

in mourning, however, his words were considered far too insensitive.

Aware of Muhammad's orders against commenting on the assassination, Nation officers present immediately alerted Muhammad of Malcolm's statement. The next day, Muhammad suspended Malcolm from the Nation for 90 days. This meant Malcolm was not allowed to teach or speak publicly.

Malcolm X traveled to Phoenix, Arizona, to meet with Muhammad, who removed him from his position as the Nation's representative. Malcolm X never officially represented the Nation again.

Malcolm X announced his resignation from the Nation on March 8, 1964. One day later, Malcolm announced he was forming a new organization, Muslim Mosque Incorporated (MMI).

CHAPTER
SEVEN

A CHANGED MAN

C hased away from the Nation of Islam, Malcolm X found himself making another change in his life. He started traveling abroad more, leaving the country four times between April 1964 and February 1965, which included two extended trips to Africa.

During the first trip, he traveled to Mecca in Saudi Arabia, where he completed his hajj, a religious pilgrimage to the Islamic holy city. Following the experience, Malcolm X returned to the United States a profoundly changed man.

New Attitude

Among the changes in Malcolm's thinking was his view of white people. Poet Maya Angelou recalled meeting Malcolm X as he made his way through Africa. Angelou said:

> When he came to Ghana and said, "I have found blue-eyed men that I am able to call brother, so my entire statement when I said all whites are devils is erroneous."

Malcolm X's travels to the Middle East and Africa in 1964 changed his worldview.

It takes an incredible amount of courage to say, say to everybody, "Remember what I said yesterday? That's wrong!" And, that's what he was able to do—that was amazing.[1]

While visiting Mecca, Malcolm learned the Islam taught under Muhammad and the Nation of Islam differed greatly from traditional Islam. He also found the religion was not strictly for black Muslims. Speaking about the mistakes of his original perceptions, Malcolm expressed a change in racial philosophies after seeing "thousands of people of different races and colors who treated me as a human being."[2]

On May 22, 1964, the day after his return from Africa, Malcolm explained his newest views at a press

TRAVELING ABROAD

Malcolm X made four international trips in the final year of his life. The highlight of the first trip was a visit to Mecca, Saudi Arabia, the holiest city in the Islamic religion. Starting on April 13, 1964, in Germany, Malcolm continued on to Saudi Arabia, Egypt, Lebanon, Liberia, Senegal, Nigeria, Algeria, and Ghana before returning home May 21.

His longest trip was from July 9 to November 24, 1964, when he visited England, Egypt, Nigeria, Tanzania, West Africa, and France. Before the year was over, Malcolm returned to England from November 30 to December 3.

Malcolm visited England, France, and Switzerland from February 5 until February 13, 1965. Malcolm was detained at the airport in France, however, and kept from traveling within the country.

conference in Chicago. He said, "Separation is not the goal of the Afro-American, nor is integration his goal. They are merely methods toward his real end—respect as a human being."[3]

New Danger

Malcolm was becoming more at ease with those he had previously assumed were his enemy. Now he had to fear his former Nation brothers. For the first time, Malcolm began speaking out publically about the paternity accusations against Muhammad. The first time he did so, Malcolm's wife, Betty, received a phone call with death threats against Malcolm the next day. Already informed once of a Nation plot to kill him, Malcolm reported to the police other situations he considered attempts on his life. Some factions within the police department disregarded

HOME ALONE

While Malcolm X traveled through Africa, he was aware his absence was taking a toll on his family. Betty was home in New York with their daughters Attallah, Qubilah, and Ilyasah.

In his hotel room while during a visit to Mecca, he wrote in his notebook:

> I know that I am surrounded by friends whose sincerity and religious zeal I can feel. I must pray again to thank Allah for this blessing, and I must pray again that my wife and children back in America will always be blessed for their sacrifices, too.[4]

While abroad, Malcolm X met with Prince Faisal al-Saud of Saudi Arabia.

Malcolm's claims, and his reports were not always
taken seriously.

Traveling gave Malcolm a reprieve from the threat
of violence at home. But while in the United States, he
began carrying tear gas pens with him for protection.
Although he denied it, he reportedly only traveled when
accompanied by a bodyguard.

Malcolm's battles with the Nation of Islam continued
on the legal front as well. He offered support to the
women suing Muhammad and was prepared to testify
in their court cases. The Nation of Islam started an
eviction process to have Malcolm removed from his

home. The Nation claimed the house had been supplied to him while he served as minister in Harlem. For the same reason, it also reclaimed Malcolm's car.

During his time with the Nation, Malcolm's necessities were covered but his actual salary was not substantial. He had not purchased many of his possessions, which created debate over what was payment for his services and what the Nation owned.

Multiple Goals

Malcolm X had many issues to deal with between 1964 and 1965. Malcolm was battling the Nation on the legal front. He was trying to continue his activism even though he was well aware his life was in jeopardy. He was still in the early stages of building two organizations—the MMI and the OAAU.

The MMI included many former Nation members. Through the MMI, Malcolm

LIVING WITH THREATS

As the threats continued, Malcolm X confided in those around him during his final days. He was aware of the murder plots surrounding him and started living out of a hotel room. He refused offers to stay with friends because he said he did not want someone else to be harmed by those coming after him. Although he made reports to police when he believed assassination attempts were made, Malcolm did not think the threats were seriously investigated.

The charred remains of furniture sit outside Malcolm X's house after it was firebombed on February 14, 1965.

said Islam could help uplift blacks through moral improvement and ending behavior destructive to the black community. Politically, Malcolm said the organization continued to follow Muhammad's philosophy of Black Nationalism.

The OAAU, which launched June 28, 1964, attempted to tackle civil rights issues. It was made up primarily of younger people who were new followers of Malcolm. Malcolm warned those joining the OAAU they could be subjecting themselves to harassment from the FBI, as well as the New York Police Department.

Fire

Malcolm X returned from a European trip on February 13, 1965. In the early morning of February 14, he awoke to Molotov cocktails crashing through the windows of his home.

As the home filled with smoke from the firebombing, Malcolm rounded up Betty and their four daughters and brought them to safety in the backyard. "I was almost frightened by his courage and efficiency in a time of terror," Betty said. "I always knew he was strong. But at that hour, I learned how great his strength was."[5] Malcolm and his family moved out of their home on February 18, hours before the eviction became official.

EL-HAJJ MALIK EL-SHABAZZ

The man born Malcolm Little, who was known as Malcolm X for most of his adulthood, had a new name again. He had changed his name to el-Hajj Malik el-Shabazz. Malcolm was using Malik el-Shabazz in some situations as early as 1957. Muhammad had used the surname Shabazz for some Nation ministers. According to Nation teaching, blacks were descendants of the ancient tribe of Shabazz.

When Malcolm signed a book contract in 1963, the contract referred to him as Malcolm Shabazz. The completion of Malcolm's hajj in 1964 led to Malcolm assuming the name of el-Hajj Malik el-Shabazz. Malcolm's wife, Betty, and their children all used the surname Shabazz.

CHAPTER
EIGHT

ASSASSINATION

Malcolm X had grown aware the Nation of Islam was plotting to have him killed. An undercover New York police officer who had infiltrated the Nation's meetings had also become aware of a planned attempt on Malcolm's life.

On February 21, 1965, Malcolm X returned to speak at the Audubon Ballroom, a site where he frequently spoke to the Harlem community. Malcolm had just been introduced to the crowd of approximately 400, which included his wife Betty and their four young daughters.

Before Malcolm could begin his speech, a disturbance broke out several rows from the stage. Two men were on their feet, arguing. People around them stood up. The only two security guards with Malcolm left the stage and headed toward the scene. Malcolm yelled to the men, "Hold it! Hold it!"[1]

From the back of the room, a smoke bomb was ignited, which added to the chaos. Amidst the confusion, a gunman rose from the front row and

Malcolm X was left vulnerable on the day of his assassination.

stepped toward Malcolm. He pulled a sawed-off shotgun from the inside of his coat, took aim, and shot Malcolm X from approximately 15 feet (4.5 m) away. The shotgun blast struck Malcolm in the left side of the chest near his heart, knocking him to the ground.

Before anyone could react, two more men stood up in the front row with handguns. They fired several more shots at Malcolm. Bedlam ensued. One of the shooters ran out of the auditorium and escaped the building through a ladies restroom. Two others headed through the crowd.

Security guard Reuben X Francis shot at one of the shooters, Thomas Hagan, wounding him in the

FAMILY IN THE CROWD

Shortly before his assassination, Malcolm had been staying at a hotel. He had asked his family not to attend his speeches, partly because of the threats surrounding him. But on the morning of February 21, 1965, Malcolm X called his wife, Betty, and surprised her by saying she and their four daughters could attend his speech that day. "And I was very happy, you know, that I could go because I had not seen him in 24 hours," Betty said.[2]

Malcolm's family was seated in the front row that day and witnessed his murder up close. At the time of his death, Malcolm X and Betty had four daughters: Attallah, Qubilah, Ilyasah, and Gamilah. The four little girls were with their mother at the Audubon when their father was murdered. But Malcolm X never met his two youngest daughters. Betty was pregnant with their twin daughters, Malaak and Malikah, who were born in late 1965, after Malcolm's death.

A crime scene photo of the Audubon Ballroom stage facing the audience, with circles indicating bullet holes on the podium where Malcolm X was standing

thigh as he tried to escape. Malcolm X's supporters began beating Hagan. He had to be pulled from the crowd by the police when they arrived and took him away from the scene. The other shooters, who had staged the diversion with the argument and set off the smoke bomb, managed to blend in with the crowd and disappeared.

Rather than wait for help, a group of supporters from Malcolm's two budding organizations, the MMI and the OAAU, ran to Columbia Presbyterian Hospital several blocks away. They returned with a stretcher, which they used to rush Malcolm to the hospital.

Doctors spent 15 minutes trying emergency measures to revive Malcolm. But at 3:30 p.m., a doctor stepped into the hospital's waiting room to deliver horrifying news to the gathering crowd. "The gentleman you knew as Malcolm X is dead," the doctor said.[3]

Questions Raised

Malcolm X had been in danger for almost a year. Now, the life of one of America's most prominent civil rights leaders was over. The former Nation minister had been left particularly vulnerable on the day he was murdered.

Despite previous threats on Malcolm's life, police were not inside the Audubon at the time of the shooting. Someone organizing the event requested that police not have such a visible presence. The police

MURDER TRIAL

Thomas Hagan, known at the time as Talmadge X. Hayer, was brought to trial along with Norman Butler and Thomas Johnson, on January 12, 1966. During the murder trial, Betty Shabazz, Malcolm X's widow, pointed to the three men and screamed, "They killed my husband."[4]

All three men were convicted of first-degree murder. Hagan signed an affidavit in 1977 stating that he and four others carried out Malcolm's murder. In the affidavit, Hagan said Butler and Johnson were not part of the group.

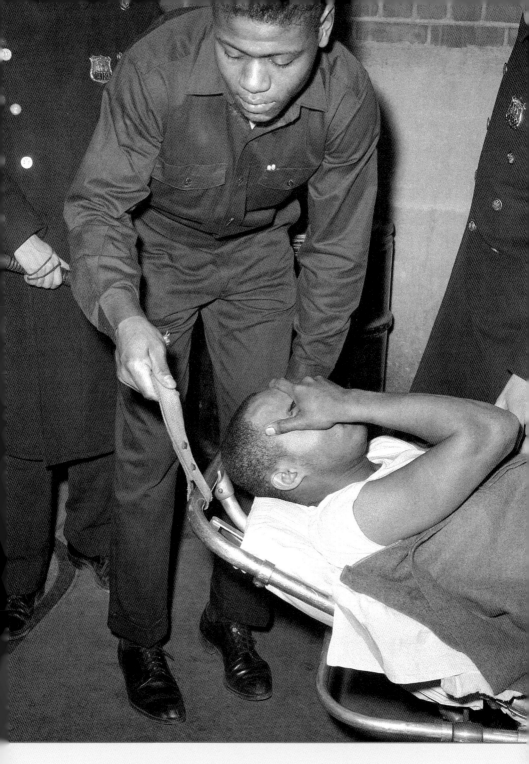

Thomas Hagan later expressed regret over shooting Malcolm X.

OFFERS OF SANCTUARY

When he was a hunted man and potential victim of assassination, Malcolm X received offers of sanctuary. Malcolm and his family were offered chances to live in Ethiopia, Saudi Arabia, and Ghana. Officials of these countries would have offered him refuge. Presumably, he would have been safer out of the reach of enemies within the Nation in the United States. Malcolm declined each offer. Friends within the United States also offered to help him hide, sometimes in their own homes. But again, Malcolm refused those offers.

moved 18 officers to the hospital nearby instead of positioning them inside the Audubon.

There had also been several changes to Malcolm's security routine, even before his last two protectors left the stage. Following the firebombing of Malcolm X's home a week earlier, members of the MMI and OAAU had planned to search every person who appeared at one of his speeches. Malcolm overruled this, as well as a measure to have more security personnel carry weapons.

Police ended their investigation of the scene at the Audubon just hours after the shooting. Because a dance was scheduled in the ballroom later that evening, police hurried the investigation. They left the crime scene cleanup to Audubon workers, who more than likely wiped away possible evidence forever.

Nation leader Muhammad went into hiding. The Nation feared retaliation from Malcolm's followers, who believed the Nation was responsible because of its feud with Malcolm. Harlem Temple No. 7, where Malcolm had previously served as minister, was set on fire two days after his assassination. Police arrested and charged Hagan, as well as two other Nation members, Norman Butler and Thomas Johnson.

The handling of the crime scene was not the only question raised about Malcolm's death. Malcolm's supporters questioned why the police had backed off from the investigation. The police had informants with inside access to all of the organizations involved. Could they have known something would happen?

Others wondered about odd steps in Malcolm's own security. He may have been betrayed by one of his own men. Many people wondered if the police even wanted to know what really happened and why they had not taken more time with the on-scene investigation. Even the suspects arrested opened questions. Some skeptics questioned whether Butler and Johnson were even there. While Hagan admitted his role, the others did not.

Other witnesses also questioned whether all responsible parties had been arrested. The argument causing the initial confusion and the smoke bomb could have each been planned distractions allowing the gunmen to get closer to Malcolm. In the years following the assassination, repeated requests for special investigations were denied.

Laid to Rest

Fears of continued violence led several churches to decline requests to host Malcolm X's funeral. The Faith Temple Church of God in Christ in West Harlem agreed to hold the funeral on February 27, 1965.

Malcolm's brothers Wilfred and Philbert did not attend the funeral. Both were still members of the Nation, and they feared becoming targets of the people who had killed their brother. "When you knew the circumstances and the kind of people that you were dealing with, you had to do your own thinking," Wilfred said. "And there was no place for me at that time."[5]

Actor and playwright Ossie Davis gave the eulogy at Malcolm's funeral. In his eulogy, Davis said:

> Many will ask what Harlem finds to honor in this stormy, controversial, and bold young captain—and we will smile . . . And we will answer and say unto them: Did

Betty Shabazz mourned her murdered husband,
who was 39 at the time of his death.

you ever talk to Brother Malcolm? Did you ever touch
him, or have him smile at you? . . . And if you knew him
you would know why we must honor him: Malcolm was
our manhood, our living black manhood! . . . And we
will know him then for what he was and is—a prince –
our own black shining prince—who didn't hesitate to die
because he loved us so.[6]

CHAPTER
NINE

THE LEGACY OF MALCOLM X

Author Alex Haley had started working with Malcolm X on Malcolm's autobiography during the last two years of the civil rights activist's life. But after Malcolm X's murder at the Audubon Ballroom, Doubleday, the book's publisher, decided to cancel the book's publication. The book had already experienced many delays.

Eventually, a new publisher, Grove Press, purchased the manuscript. Before 1965 was over, *The Autobiography of Malcolm X* was published. More than 6 million copies of the autobiography sold between 1965 and 1977.

Even in the aftermath of his murder, media descriptions of Malcolm X were highly critical. He had lived such a controversial life that even as a victim of crime, he was the subject of harsh commentary.

The release of his autobiography, however, helped some readers and the media have a better understanding

Malcolm X and his views have been the subject of many books and films.

of Malcolm X. Despite his controversial methods to create societal change for blacks, Malcolm's popularity rose after his death. Many more books, in part or in whole, sought to explain Malcolm's complex views and life.

Family

After his death, Malcolm's widow, Betty Shabazz, remained committed to raising their six daughters, including the twins who were born after his death. She also continued her own education.

Betty also frequently lectured about civil rights issues. She died in 1997, three weeks after suffering severe burns over 80 percent of her body from a fire set by her grandson.

But Malcolm's family did not escape some of the violence and controversy surrounding his death. Malcolm and Betty's daughter Qubilah was charged with trying to arrange the murder of Louis Farrakhan in 1995. Farrakhan became the head of the Nation of

Author Alex Haley interviewed Malcolm X up
until Malcolm's death in 1965.

Islam and Betty had believed Farrakhan participated in
the conspiracy to murder Malcolm. Qubilah eventually
agreed to a deal with federal prosecutors to avoid a trial
and possible 90-year prison sentence.

The Movie

Director Spike Lee released his film *Malcolm X* in 1992,
and it was based heavily on the autobiography. Starring

ALEX HALEY

Starting in 1963, Haley conducted dozens of interviews with Malcolm X, which eventually produced *The Autobiography of Malcolm X*. Haley was also honored for his other works on African-American history in the United States. He received the 1977 Pulitzer Prize as author of *Roots: The Saga of an American Family,* which was published in 1976.

actor Denzel Washington, the movie features the life of the former Nation of Islam minister.

The film was well received by critics, including Roger Ebert. "Watching the film, I understood more clearly how we do have the power to change our own lives, how fate doesn't deal all of the cards," Ebert said.[1]

It also impacted preconceptions of Malcolm, even 27 years after his death. "Malcolm X was a far more complicated figure than any of us knew in the '60s," said Robert O'Meally, an American Studies professor at Barnard College in New York, when the film was released. "If you look at the whole range of his career, you can see some pretty good Malcolms in the barrel with the bad ones."[2]

While the film was only in production, sales of *The Autobiography of Malcolm X* again climbed, as well as collections of Malcolm X's speeches. Black hats with a simple *X* became increasingly popular in many urban areas. The expanding hip-hop culture of the 1990s contained frequent references to Malcolm X.

More to Learn

Many people began to see Malcolm X in a different light in the decades following his death. The Nation of Islam also remembered his contributions, despite his falling-out with its former minister and accusations of the organization's involvement in his murder.

Elijah Muhammad's son Wallace took control of the Black Muslim organization after the death of his father in 1975. A year after taking over leadership, Wallace

MALCOLM X

For his film portrayal of Malcolm X, Denzel Washington was nominated for an Oscar for Best Actor in a Leading Role at the 1993 Academy Awards. Washington also received a nomination for Best Performance by an Actor in a Motion Picture–Drama at the 1993 Golden Globe Awards.

Malcolm X and Washington were recognized at the 1993 NAACP Image Awards. The Image Awards recognize achievements by people of color in literature, television, music, and film. *Malcolm X* won Outstanding Motion Picture, and Washington received Outstanding Actor in a Motion Picture. Angela Bassett, who played Betty Shabazz, received Outstanding Supporting Actress, and Al Freeman Jr. won the Outstanding Supporting Actor award for his portrayal of Elijah Muhammad.

Malcolm X inspired other Black Power movements.

announced the Harlem Temple No. 7, where Malcolm X
had once been minister, would be renamed as the El-
Hajj Malik El-Shabazz Mosque in his honor.

Countless buildings and streets have also been
renamed in Malcolm X's honor. Malcolm X was also
memorialized with a stamp issued by the US Postal
Service in 1999.

Following his death, Malcolm X's ideas and speeches
became particularly popular among black youth during
the civil rights movement. His teachings became the

inspiration for other Black Nationalist groups, such as the Black Panther Party, which first formed in 1966. Those who felt deprived of opportunity spoke out about the need for change rather than just hoping for it to happen.

Almost a half-century after his death, Malcolm X's legacy continues. In 2011, scholar Manning Marable released *Malcolm X: A Life of Reinvention*, a controversial, 594-page biography. After the release of Marable's book, analysis of some of his revelations began. The book raised questions about the accuracy of specific aspects of Malcolm's autobiography. Malcolm's daughters took exception to Marable's portrayal of problems within the marriage of Malcolm and Betty Shabazz and the possibility of extramarital relationships.

Malcolm X's 39 years were too complex to easily summarize. His ideas, actions, and speeches are still debated. During the last years of his life, Malcolm X displayed an ability to change and expand his views, and fight for human rights, rather than solely civil rights. His willingness to embrace controversy while loudly demanding better treatment of blacks left a lasting impact on the civil rights movement.

TIMELINE

1925
Malcolm Little is born to Earl and Louise Little on May 19, in Omaha, Nebraska.

1931
Earl Little Sr. dies on September 28 after he is run over by a streetcar.

1939
Louise Little is committed to a state mental hospital in Kalamazoo, Michigan, on January 31.

1940
Malcolm drops out of high school before finishing the ninth grade.

1941
In February, Malcolm moves to Boston, Massachusetts, to live with his half sister Ella Collins.

1946
Malcolm is arrested and begins serving a prison sentence in Charlestown, Massachusetts, on February 27.

1952
Malcolm is released from prison on August 7.

1952
Malcolm joins the Nation of Islam and changes his name to Malcolm X.

1953
Malcolm X becomes the first minister of the Nation's Boston Temple No. 11.

1954
Malcolm X becomes chief minister of Harlem's Temple No. 7 in June.

1958
Malcolm X marries Betty Sanders in Lansing, Michigan, on January 14.

TIMELINE

1961
Muhammad makes Malcolm X the Nation of Islam's national representative.

1963
The Nation suspends Malcolm X for 90 days after his disrespectful remarks about President John F. Kennedy's assassination.

1964
Malcolm X resigns from the Nation of Islam on March 8. He forms the Muslim Mosque Incorporated (MMI) on March 9.

1964
On March 26, Malcolm X meets Dr. Martin Luther King Jr. for the first and only time in Washington, DC.

1964
Malcolm delivers his "The Ballot or the Bullet" speech on April 3 in Ohio.

1964

Malcolm X visits Mecca, Saudi Arabia,
one of Islam's holiest cities, in April.

1964

Malcolm X announces the formation of the Organization
of Afro-American Unity (OAAU) on June 28.

1965

On February 14, Malcolm X and his family escape
a firebombing of their Queens, New York, home.

1965

On February 21, Malcolm X is assassinated
at the Audubon Ballroom in Harlem.

1965

Funeral services for Malcolm X are held
in New York City on February 27.

ESSENTIAL FACTS

Date of Birth
May 19, 1925

Place of Birth
Omaha, Nebraska

Date of Death
February 21, 1965

Parents
Earl and Louise Little

Education
Left high school before finishing ninth grade. Finished high school diploma while in prison in Massachusetts.

Marriage
Betty Sanders (January 14, 1958)

Children
Daughters Attallah, Qubilah, Ilyasah, Gamilah, Malaak, and Malikah

Career Highlights
Malcolm X transformed his life of crime and became a charismatic minister and national spokesman for the Nation of Islam. Through his work with the Nation, he supported Black Nationalism during the growing civil rights movement.

After breaking away from the Nation of Islam, he founded the Muslim Mosque Incorporated and Organization of Afro-American Unity. Malcolm X changed his worldview and worked to achieve human rights worldwide.

Societal Contributions

Malcolm X spread Islam to blacks, encouraging them to have racial pride and independence. He encouraged his followers to reject behavior destructive to black communities. He was an inspiration for blacks who were unhappy with the progress of mainstream civil rights groups, as well as future civil rights groups.

Conflicts

Malcolm X called for Black Nationalism, the opposite of mainstream civil rights leaders who fought for equality within the power structure. He controversially advocated for blacks to use violence when necessary to defend themselves against mistreatment of white Americans. After he was ousted from the Nation of Islam, he was at odds with his former allies, who conspired to assassinate him in 1965.

Quote

"We're not Americans. We're Africans who happen to be in America. We were kidnapped and brought here against our will from Africa. We didn't land on Plymouth Rock—that rock landed on us."—*Malcolm X*

GLOSSARY

activist
Someone who protests or speaks out against a social, political, economic, or moral wrong.

adultery
Voluntary sex between a married person and someone who is not his or her spouse. Also referred to as infidelity.

assassination
The murder of a well-known person.

charisma
The special ability of a leader to persuade or influence others.

conspiracy
A secret plot between individuals to commit an illegal act.

discrimination
Treating a person differently because of the group to which he or she belongs.

integration
The bringing together of different groups into a blended group.

Molotov cocktail
Explosive device typically consisting of a bottle with gasoline and a rag used to light it before it is thrown.

racism
The belief race determines inherent differences and one race is superior to another.

retaliation
Revenge.

segregation
The separation of one racial group from another or from society.

sentencing
The issuing of a prison term.

white supremacy
The belief that the white race is superior to all others.

ADDITIONAL RESOURCES

Selected Bibliography

Cone, James. *Martin & Malcolm & America: A Dream or a Nightmare*. New York: Orbis, 1991. Print.

Malcolm X, as told to Alex Haley. *The Autobiography of Malcolm X*. New York: Ballantine, 1999. Print.

Malcolm X. *By Any Means Necessary: Speeches, Interviews, and a Letter by Malcolm X*. New York: Pathfinder, 1970. Print.

Further Readings

Gormley, Beatrice. *Malcolm X: A Revolutionary Voice*. New York: Sterling, 2008. Print.

Marable, Manning. *Malcolm X: A Life of Reinvention*. New York: Penguin, 2011. Print.

Pinkney, Andrea. *Hand in Hand: Ten Black Men Who Changed America*. New York: Hyperion, 2012. Print.

Web Sites

To learn more about Malcolm X, visit ABDO Publishing Company online at **www.abdopublishing.com**. Web sites about Malcolm X are featured on our Book Links page. These links are routinely monitored and updated to provide the most current information available.

Places to Visit

Malcolm X Birthsite

3448 Evans Street
Omaha, NE 68111
402-881-8118
http://malcolmxfoundation.org/wp
The Malcolm X Memorial Foundation remembers Malcolm
X with a plaza and educational memorial at the site of his
birth.

The Malcolm X & Dr. Betty Shabazz Memorial and Educational Center

3940 Broadway Avenue
New York City, NY 10032
212-568-1341
http://theshabazzcenter.net
This center is dedicated to Malcolm X and his wife, Betty,
and located on the former site of the Audubon Ballroom.

The National Museum of African American History and Culture

1400 Constitution Avenue NW
Washington, DC 20004
http://nmaahc.si.edu
Located within the Smithsonian's Museum of American
History, this museum provides exhibits on African-American
culture and history. Construction on a new National
Museum of African American History and Culture building
began in 2012 and is scheduled for completion in 2015.

SOURCE NOTES

Chapter 1. By Any Means Necessary

1. "(1964) Malcolm X's Speech at the Founding Rally of the Organization of Afro-American Unity | The Black Past: Remembered and Reclaimed." *BlackPast.org*. BlackPast.org, n.d. Web. 20 Nov. 2012.

2. Ibid.

3. Ibid.

4. Ibid.

5. Ibid.

6. Ibid.

Chapter 2. Volatile Childhood

1. "Transcript: Malcolm X: Make It Plain." *PBS*. PBS, 19 May 2005. Web. 24 Apr. 2013.

2. Malcolm X and Alex Haley. *The Autobiography of Malcolm X*. New York: Ballantine, 1998. Print. 7.

3. Manning Marable. *Malcolm X: A Life of Reinvention*. New York: Penguin, 2012. Print. 38.

Chapter 3. Life of Crime

1. "Malcolm X Biography." *Bio.com*. A&E Networks Television, n.d. Web. 23 Dec. 2012.

Chapter 4. The Nation of Islam

1. Joby Waldman. "Misunderstanding Malcolm X." *BBC News*. BBC, 21 Feb. 2005. Web. 26 Dec. 2012.

2. Adam Pachter. "Any Means Necessary." *PBS*. PBS, 19 May 2005. Web. 25 Dec. 2012.

3. Manning Marable. *Malcolm X: A Life of Reinvention*. New York: Penguin, 2012. Print. 113.

4. Ibid.

5. Adam Pachter. "Any Means Necessary." *PBS*. PBS, 19 May 2005. Web. 25 Dec. 2012.

6. Manning Marable. *Malcolm X: A Life of Reinvention*. New York: Penguin, 2012. Print. 127–129.

Chapter 5. Opposing Messages

1. Manning Marable. *Malcolm X: A Life of Reinvention*. New York: Penguin, 2012. Print. 198.

2. Alex Haley. "Alex Haley Interviews Martin Luther King, Jr. (January 1965)." *Playboy* Jan. 1965. *Alex-Haley.com*. Web. 23 May 2013.

3. Claude Lewis. "Malcolm X on Life, Death and the Struggle." *Philly.com*. Philly.com, 18 Nov. 1992. Web. 26 Dec. 2012.

4. John Blake. "Malcolm and Martin, Closer Than We Ever Thought." *CNN*. CNN, 19 May 2010. Web. 26 Dec. 2012.

5. Malcolm X and Alex Haley. *The Autobiography of Malcolm X*. New York: Ballantine, 1998. Print. 385.

6. Ibid.

7. John Blake. "Malcolm and Martin, Closer Than We Ever Thought." *CNN*. CNN, 19 May 2010. Web. 26 Dec. 2012.

8. "Malcolm X: The Ballot or the Bullet." *Malcolm X: The Ballot or the Bullet*. EdChange, n.d. Web. 24 Apr. 2013.

9. Manning Marable. *Malcolm X: A Life of Reinvention*. New York: Penguin, 2012. Print. 304.

Chapter 6. Growing Tensions

1. Manning Marable. *Malcolm X: A Life of Reinvention*. New York: Penguin, 2012. Print. 171.

2. Ibid. 212.

3. Ibid. 212.

4. Ibid. 216.

5. "Transcript: Malcolm X: Make It Plain." *PBS*. PBS, 19 May 2005. Web. 24 Apr. 2013.

6. Manning Marable. *Malcolm X: A Life of Reinvention*. New York: Penguin, 2012. Print. 258–259.

7. Ibid., 247.

8. "Malcolm X Biography." *Encyclopedia of World Biography*. Advameg, n.d. Web. 24 Apr. 2013.

9. Manning Marable. *Malcolm X: A Life of Reinvention*. New York: Penguin, 2012. Print. 272–273.

10. Peter Dreier. "The Greatest—Muhammad Ali—Turns 70." *The Huffington Post*. TheHuffingtonPost.com, 17 Jan. 2012. Web. 24 Apr. 2013.

SOURCE NOTES CONTINUED

Chapter 7. A Changed Man

1. Joby Waldman. "Misunderstanding Malcolm X." *BBC News*. BBC, 21 Feb. 2005. Web. 26 Dec. 2012.

2. Manning Marable. *Malcolm X: A Life of Reinvention*. New York: Penguin, 2012. Print. 319, 323.

3. Ibid. 332.

4. Malcolm X and Alex Haley. *The Autobiography of Malcolm X*. New York: Ballantine, 1998. Print. 341.

5. Manning Marable. *Malcolm X: A Life of Reinvention*. New York: Penguin, 2012. Print. 415–416.

Chapter 8. Assassination

1. Malcolm X and Alex Haley. *The Autobiography of Malcolm X*. New York: Ballantine, 1998. Print. 442–443.

2. "Transcript: Malcolm X: Make It Plain." *PBS*. PBS, 19 May 2005. Web. 24 Apr. 2013.

3. Manning Marable. *Malcolm X: A Life of Reinvention*. New York: Penguin, 2012. Print. 436–441.

4. Mark Jacobson. "The Man Who Didn't Shoot Malcolm X." *New York Magazine*. New York Media, 30 Sept. 2007. Web. 24 Apr. 2013.

5. "Transcript: Malcolm X: Make It Plain." *PBS*. PBS, 19 May 2005. Web. 24 Apr. 2013.

6. Malcolm X and Alex Haley. *The Autobiography of Malcolm X*. New York: Ballantine, 1998. Print. 461–462.

Chapter 9. The Legacy of Malcolm X

1. Roger Ebert. "Malcolm X." *RogerEbert.com*. Ebert Digital, 18 Nov. 1992. Web. 24 Apr. 2013.

2. Lewis Lord, Jeannye Thornton, and Alejando Bodipo-Memba. "The Legacy of Malcolm X." *U.S. News & World Report*. U.S. News & World Report, 15 Nov. 1992. Web. 26 Dec. 2012.

INDEX

ABOUT THE AUTHOR

Tom Robinson is a freelance writer and editor from Clarks Summit, Pennsylvania. During his career as a sports writer, Tom received national honors from the Associated Press Sports Editors and state awards from the Pennsylvania Newspaper Publishers Association. He is the author of 34 books, including biographies of prominent figures in US history for young readers.

ABOUT THE CONSULTANT

Dr. Alan Bloom is an Associate Professor of History at Valparaiso University in Valparaiso, Indiana. He received a bachelor of arts from the University of California at Santa Barbara and a PhD from Duke University. He has research interests in the history of homelessness, urban America, sports, and civil rights. He has written essays on homelessness, Malcolm X, and urban renewal in Valparaiso.